The Gift of Delay:

Selected Poems

Maja Vidmar

THE GIFT OF DELAY

SELECTED POEMS

Translated from the Slovenian by Andrej Pleterski

DALKEY ARCHIVE PRESS

Library of Congress Cataloging-in-Publication Data
Names: Vidmar, Maja, 1961- author. | Pleterski, Andrej, translator.
Title: The gift of delay : selected poems / Maja Vidmar ; translated by Andrej
Pleterski
Description: First Dalkey archive edition. | Victoria, TX : Dalkey
Archive Press, 2017. | Translation from Slovenian into English.
Identifiers: LCCN 2017032908 | ISBN 9781943150298 (pbk. : alk. paper)
Subjects: LCSH: Vidmar, Maja, 1961---Translations into English.
Classification: LCC PG1919.32.I3 .A2 2017 | DDC 891.8/415--dc23
LC record available at https://lccn.loc.gov/2017032908

www.dalkeyarchive.com
Victoria, TX / McLean, IL / Dublin

SLOVENIAN
BOOK
AGENCY

Društvo slovenskih pisateljev
Slovene Writers' Association

LITTERÆ
SLOVENICÆ
Slovenian Literary Magazine

This translation has been financially supported by the Slovenian Book Agency.

Published in cooperation with the Slovene Writers' Association – Litteræ
Slovenicæ Series.

This work has been published with the support of the Trubar Foundation,
located at the Slovene Writers' Association, Ljubljana, Slovenia.

Dalkey Archive Press publications are, in part, made possible through the
support of the University of Houston-Victoria and its programs in creative
writing, publishing, and translation

Printed on permanent/durable acid-free paper

Contents

A DIALOGUE WITH MAJA VIDMAR'S POETRY

Peter Semolič

THE 1970S AND most of the 1980s were dominated in Slovenian poetry by modernism, which was intensely involved with language at several levels, sonority as well as morphology and syntax. At the same time, the mid-seventies already witnessed the emergence of poets whose poetic practice diverged in many respects from the established approach. These authors replaced their predecessors' "transmental" idiom with a more direct one, an idiom which, to put it simply, (re)enabled them to express in verse the world and themselves within that world. One of the strongest and most distinct poetic voices of the then-younger generation certainly belonged to Maja Vidmar.

Maja Vidmar, born in 1961 at Nova Gorica, a town by the Slovenian-Italian border, lives as a freelance poet in Ljubljana, Slovenia. She has published seven poetry collections in Slovenian and as many in translation, her poetry has been included in approximately seventy anthologies worldwide. Her work has been recognized with a number of national and international prizes. The former include the highest honor for a book of poetry in Slovenia, the Jenko Award, and the national award for literature and art, the Prešeren Foundation Award, for her collection *Presence* (*Prisotnost*), as well as the award Velenjica—Cup of Immortality (*Velenjica—čaša nesmrtnosti*), which marks a decade of outstanding poetic work. Her international prizes include the Hubert Burda Foundation Prize for Young Poets (Offenburg, Germany), the Umberto Saba Award at the international poetry contest Trieste Scritture di Frontiera (Trieste, Italy), and the Prize of the Network of Literary Cities (*Nagrada mreže gradova književnosti*, Pazin, Croatia). In addition, she received a Vienna scholarship in the framework of the Großer Preis für osteuropäische Literatur.

Maja Vidmar attracted the notice of critics and readers with her very first poetry collection, *Distances of the Body* (*Razdalje telesa*, 1984). As the title suggests, the poems in *Distances of the Body* take place in the field of the intimate, with an emphasis on physicality and on the coming together and moving apart of two bodies, male and female. Contemporary criticism classified the collection as predominantly erotic poetry, which it certainly is, but it must be noted that eroticism has never been merely a physical issue for Vidmar: the poetry in *Distances of the Body* is often permeated by intense, borderline emotions, such as pain, fear, or jealousy. An important prefiguration of her subsequent poetic trajectory is the cycle of poems written as a dialogue between lovers, since it is precisely dialogue, as this essay will show, that forms a central characteristic of her poetry.

In her next two poetry collections, *Ways of Binding* (*Način vezave*, 1988) and *At the Base* (*Ob vznožju*, 1998), Vidmar significantly expanded "both the thematic and aesthetic dimensions of her debut," according to the poet Niko Grafenauer. The poems grow more dissonant, introducing new themes and motifs. Roughly speaking, *Ways of Binding* explores alienation, a world in which a love relationship between two people is merely one of the many possible ways of connection, and as such for many reasons and in many respects arbitrary. The collection *At the Base*, on the other hand, addresses subjection, either to a man or to God, which implies inequality. Thus Vidmar's poetry gradually loses its intimate character and comes to embrace distinct social themes as well, such as the theme of war in *At the Base*.

The trio of Maja Vidmar's early poetry collections left a substantial imprint on the Slovenian poetry scene. Indeed, it was her work that established women's verse on the map of contemporary Slovenian literature: even while her poetry, like the poetry of her fellow women authors, still tended to be addressed in Slovenian criticism as a "variant of male poetry," that label was being increasingly placed in parentheses. For various historical and cultural reasons, women poets had been an exception rather

than the rule in Slovenian literature, and the image of woman
in literary texts had largely reflected the traditional notions of
woman and her role in society. This view teetered in the 1980s,
when Slovenian society began to foster individual identities
in addition to the dominant national identity. The process of
society diversification was somewhat slowed down by Slovenia's
break away from Yugoslavia, which called for the unification of
male and female citizens on a national basis, but it could not be
stopped. The issue of partial identities was foregrounded again at
the close of the millennium. From this perspective, too, a sem-
inal poetry collection of the period was Maja Vidmar's *Presence*
(*Prisotnost*, 2005).

The poetry book *Presence* (2005), which opens the present
selection, represents a watershed in the author's oeuvre. Although
Maja Vidmar remains a lyric poet, that is, an author of short
poetic texts polished to verbal perfection, there are major shifts
within the narrowly circumscribed space of the poems. If her
previous poetry was characterized by a relatively frequent use of
rhyme and assonance, thus occasionally evoking the rhythms of
folk songs, rhyme and assonance give way in her recent poems
to a more pronounced free verse, which slows down and relaxes
the rhythm, at the same time reinforcing and sharpening it. The
language register is lowered: her poetry, which has up to now,
especially through aposiopesis and omission, owed much to the
modernist ideal of a "self-referential poem," is invaded by every-
day speech. "Make use of ordinary words / and used-up meta-
phors / the way I use them," she writes in the poem "Devices."
And with the coming of everyday phrases, her poetry is deci-
sively infiltrated by social considerations. According to literary
critic and poet Petra Koršič, the poems from *Presence* can be
described in relation to Vidmar's previous poetry as "a shift
from microcosm to macrocosm, whereby the poet moves from
private to public." Gender, never limited in her poetry to the
biological gender alone, begins to grow with *Presence* into a social
gender as well. Eroticism, the soil from which the bulk of her

poetry springs, thus transcends the intimacy between two lovers, expanding into a field in which "dramas" are enacted between various social roles. Maja Vidmar's poetry evolves into a distinct dialogue between various characters and *personae*, who are almost always portrayed in their relation to others: the reader thus encounters a woman among women, a woman among men, a woman in the role of a partner or mother, etc.

The collection *Rooms* (*Sobe*, 2008) seems to suggest the poet's return to the first-person narrative, but this return may well be specious: according to literary critic and writer Lucija Stepančič, "the impression prevails that it is all happening to a variety of people in a variety of circumstances." Like Vidmar's other collections, the book is meticulously arranged to form a gathering of rooms as well as of other spaces, such as cellars, bomb shelters, or tunnels, which witness the intimate dramas enacted within and between the protagonists of the various poems. Being scheduled for full-length publication in English, however, the collection *Rooms* is not included in our selection.

In her collection *How You Fall In Love* (*Kako se zaljubiš*, 2012), Vidmar takes a step further, positioning herself in a love relationship with various objects, material or immaterial—a child, death, herself, a beloved man—as well as with the past and future, dog and man, and more. Thus her poetry often reaches beyond social roles, shedding new, surprising light on the objects of her poems and on their mutual relationships. Her next collection, *A Minute Head Start* (*Minute prednosti*, 2015), takes as its point of departure social labels, curious as to what lies beyond them.

In *A Minute Head Start* the poet again plays through a variety of roles, which has by now become her distinctive feature. The poems take place in a socially and culturally marked intimacy, the writing springs from the subject's deep, erotic, well-nigh tactile attitude to the world. This is highlighted in the very first poem of the collection, "The Drumroll Rehearsal": "Be a robin / fluttering off onto a thin branch / of the flute, and a flutist / holding her breath. / Then breathe through all / the possible swaps / . . . " Her use of the *persona* significantly departs from that in her earlier collections. At first the speakers are animals, but not in the tradition of animal fables. While the poet admittedly cannot help humanizing them somewhat by the very act of placing words into their mouths or beaks, she also recognizes the uniqueness of their relation to the human world. Continually addressing the subject, the animals in this collection evade the established use of the *persona* as well as repeatedly turn the subject into object. This use of the *persona*, an innovation in terms of poetry, results in a world which is no longer anthropocentric but centers on animals rather than humans: on a scorpion, fishes, a fawn, and others. A parallel process is the decentralization of the subject, particularly evident in the poems featuring allegorical figures which express certain aspects of the psyche, such as "the Worrisome Man," "the Sorrowful Man," or "the Cynical Man."

What is enacted before us, then, is a drama of decentralization—first of the world and then of the subject. The world is unstable, crumbling into images which are no less unstable, porous. A similar fate befalls the subject, dismembered into individual functions with which the "I" is in perpetual dialog. This dialogue, however, seems riddled with misunderstandings and accompanied by a silent struggle to control the functioning of the disintegrating subject, a subject which dissolves by the end of the book into a dialog of undefined and unidentified voices. No animals or allegoric figures are left to lend shape to the voices talking past each other, or to offer them the shelter of the—at least partly—familiar. The subject, which has up to this moment maintained a certain transparency to itself and to the reader, which has still been capable of talking about being "lost," is now truly lost. "Who are you?" is a question obsessively repeated throughout the concluding poems of *A Minute Head Start*, while the replies lack any clear starting-point or clear reference: they are but a multitude of voices quavering on the edge of the hearing field. Beginning with the "swaps," continuing with disintegration of the anthropocentric world and dismemberment of the subject, the collection fades out into formlessness and solitude.

Indeed, it is this basic mood of solitude that pervades Maja Vidmar's latest poems, gathered in the present edition under the heading "A Child and Other Phenomena." These poems boldly continue to develop certain aspects of her poetics. A case in point is her handling of animals. Animals feature in her early poetry as well, but mostly for the qualities which supposedly connect them to the human world. The collection *How You Fall In Love*, on the other hand, introduces an important gap between subject and animal: the animal may symbolize innocence or "a healed world," but it is already in the process of becoming mostly itself, that is, something different from us. This process of animals' "emancipation" from our notions about them reaches a new phase in the *A Minute Head Start* poems: here, the animals already are the Other but continue as *personae* as well. In the latest poems, however, the animals fully emancipate themselves, becoming an absolute Other. Indeed, their acts as documented on our part run counter to our established notions about them, dumbly confronting us with the question: Who are they? And through that question with another, the one encountered at the conclusion of *A Minute Head Start*: *Who are you?* This question has never been limited to self-examination, never intended solely for the subject or the author: it has always addressed us readers, too. Who are you—beyond all the roles you play, beyond the labels assigned to you, who are you in relation to the human, and not merely human, world?

It is this question that seems to lie at the core, or at least very close to the core, of Maja Vidmar's poetry. It recurs again and again, always in a new way: sometimes through metaphor, sometimes directly, sometimes through the use of a *persona* or a startling change of perspective. Rather than from an identity crisis, the question springs from her perceptive contemplation of the self and of language. By contemplating herself and language, she also contemplates the Other, establishing a relation to the Other—a relation which enables her to contemplate society as a whole. And this contemplation of society reveals to her both her own self and language in a new light. Last but not least, this question springs from contemplation of the human world, which leads to contemplation of the animal world, which in its turn again leads to contemplation of the human world.

The poetry of Maja Vidmar is a poetry of relation(ship)s obtaining between different entities and different aspects of the same entity. While her poetry addresses communication and is communicative itself, it is at the same time evasive, elusive: providing no answers, it nevertheless knows how to pose the right question, again and again, at the right time and in the right place.

Lavrica, May 20, 2017

Translated by Nada Grošelj

The Gift of Delay:

Selected Poems

PRESENCE (2005)

THE HOUSE

With father's milk
I drank the solid
architecture
of the house,
but even in those rooms,
I'd cover up my head
at night, and there's
no doubt:
out in the open,
they'd come, those
who don't exist,
and devour me.

It's hard with a house
in your head.
In the evening, I go and sit
on the threshold
at the back door
and wail,
calling those
who don't exist.

TO MY DAUGHTER

Someday we'll lead
the tiger into the valley.
It will lie in the open
doorway, lending us
its gold.

Yet now, right now
I cannot sleep faced with
the fate of the snake lines,
when it skids again
across your cradle.

If it weren't for you,
you bet I'd be fleeing
in horror again, for the gullet
is haunted night and day
by the odor of the devoured.

Sleepless, I'm learning,
learning to embrace it,
so that someday we'll lead it,
the tiger into the valley.

ISAAC

When Isaac is asleep,
I cover his little wings,
I watch him breathe
and smell him
as though he were mine.
When Isaac waves to me,
I warn him, crossing
the street, shivering
as though he were mine.
For I let him go, knocking
on wood three times
every day, I let him go
among wild beasts.

How can I say it
as though I didn't care,
Isaac, come, let's climb
the mountain high.
How can I seek a block,
a chopping block, smooth
and clean just for him.
How can I take a knife,
as though I didn't care,
take a knife, gray and bare,
how can I cut him off
alive.

Isaac, come, let's go.

DEAD POEMS

Such a beautiful baby
I fed from
my round breast,
such warm milk
quenched his tender thirst
that I forgot
how inexplicably
I'd been ashamed of breastfeeding,
not wanting, truly
not wanting another baby.

Still, not the baby itself,
it's the infallibility of the dreamy
metaphor that terrifies me,
and all those dreams
about premature infants,
the little pale half-corpses,
and the pocket babies
I've abandoned
the way nobody
should abandon a baby.

NIGREDO

Before the window pane,
a wild janitor
is cutting
little black paws.
Dismembered wolves
scattered all over
are fertilizing
the school garden.
I'm running away
not to be noticed
by the merciless gardener
behind the window pane.

ALBEDO

The whiteness
of a cold night.
A swift little beast
resting its
fear.
My little red paw
dwells in
an iron trap.
Moonlight
and three footprints
in the snow.
That way.

THE TASTE OF A RAINBOW

At this very moment
a rainbow is shining
on the cup
and my warm
tea.

Curiously bent
I'm slurping it noisily
from the top of the tea,
and everything has been
like this from time
immemorial.

THE PRAYER OF AN ORANGE

If you appoint
an observer for me,
I'll be perfect in a second.
With the color and the shape
of the sun, I'll excite him
ruthlessly
in between my crescents.
You know he's never
endured perfection,
thus, at his very first cut,
I will waft
like you said once
only oranges
can waft.
Don't worry, only by
counting all my
roe, will he be immortal.

THE PRAYER OF THE NIGHT

Viewed from above,
what's more beautiful than
the flashing river of light
on the wet road.
Viewed up close,
what's more beautiful than
a sleeping little girl
in the back seat.
Viewed from where
I'm not there,
there is only darkness.

THE TINY PRAYER OF A TITMOUSE

The more it hurts me,
the sicker I'll be,
the more I mourn,
the more desperate I'll be,
the more I'm scared,
the more paralyzed I'll be,
the more offended I feel,
the greater my weight,
the more I look back,
the more I'll bump into things,
the more I daydream,
the more I'll delay,
the more I keep delaying,
the wearier I'll be,
the more I hurry,
the greater my age,
the more I miss something,
the more deprived I'll be.

Just to take off and fly.

A FLUTE

It's written down,
yet if it didn't make
me so happy,
I wouldn't want
to believe I am,
at best,
only just
a hollow enough
bone.

THE MAGPIE

When something
shines up on the sidewalk
or down in the grass,
it strikes me as if
it were here what
I might have been
looking for all this time.
Everything will be different
from now on.
When I turn around
a shard or a can
with my foot,
the reflection fades,
but the hope
keeps on fading
for a while longer.

THE SHOOTING STAR

You know
how I need
that shooting star.

My neck aches,
my legs are cold
and I'm afraid of
the bush approaching
in the dark.

Give me the star
to return into the house
to find the light
and the warmth
and to lock twice.

Give me the star,
it will be easier then.

PRESENCE

As it's being cut down,
the pine stands.

It doesn't even think
of running down the road
with its ripped-out
muddy roots.

As it's being cut down,
it's a tree at its treest.

THE COUPLE

We're alone
on a lonely island.
Waiting for a ship
that may not arrive.
We're alone,
a woman and a man.
He's nothing special
and I'm not into specialties
anyway, but there's
no choice on the island,
neither for me nor for him.

We're alone
on a lonely island.
Put on the rack
between yes and no every day.
Each day is worse
than sex.
Worst of all is my fear
of catching sight of a ship
and having to leave the shore
in the middle of the movie.
Each day is the gift
of delay.

THE FINAL ROOM

My husband is a murderer,
this has become
absolutely clear, and
threatened are the lives
of my girlfriends
and my own.
I'll betray him
as early as today, regardless
of my great shame
and the shame of
my family, but how should I
pull this off so that
he doesn't slay me
and fling me into the final

room.

WHOSE ROOM

Like a canopy torn to shreds
the bloated carcass
is finely secreting mucus
under the ceiling,
above the bed,
and the swarming mice are
sliding like sand from the head
of the bed onto the blanket.
Is this really
my room and my
bed under the ceiling?
I apologize a thousand times,
but I'll leave
nonetheless.

HERE I AM

Thank you for evoking me,
sonny, for calling me
by name, for asking
where are you.
Because when I say
here I am,
just sleep, little froglet, just sleep,
my body is sketched
in the air and my breath exchanges,
and when the soles of my feet
sprout from the ground, I'm free to go.
Thank you for evoking me,
sonny, just sleep on.

AN IDYLL

It's no coincidence that
the two of us and our kids
ended up in an elevator.
Even when I was little,
the best of all was the time
we spent in the car
with everyone within
arm's reach. The cabin
cracked like
a fresh sugar wafer,
it's all right it's all right,
we said to our two kids,
and, indeed, it didn't hurt.
A moment earlier,
I'd been thankful for
the experience.

I
THE WINTER POEM

A sword lying
in the shallows,
its flat tip
in the water of sand,
its hilt
slightly floating
in the water of silt.
It flashes at times
as it laps toward
the cold shore.
The heroes hurrying,
only children sensing
something in the water.

II
SPRING

They've never been
so drawn
to the shore.
Ecstatic, the women are
bringing clean laundry,
laying it across
the open water-lilies,
at the foot of those
walking on the water
for the first time.
Some of them claim
a great sunken heart
has started to bloom.

III
THE LAST SUMMER

The water hadn't even cooled down
at night when
the last heroes began to arrive.
It's hard to explain
that sound, but slowly they
cut up all the children
even though they were
so many one could weave
soft rafts from their little fingers
and their fine hair. By the morning,
the heroes seemed to be hugging, yet
they were only pulling out their own
young hearts into the baking silt.

IV
THE AUTUMN POEM

The lake
has assumed
its genuine image.
Everything's here,
but nothing to be seen
with their ailing eyes.
If it weren't all the same,
they could admire
the original flicker of mists.
On the raft, a few
old women
are learning to read,
from memory.

DEVICES

Make use of ordinary words
and used-up metaphors
the way I use them.
Make use of the betrayed loves
and the bloody drooping hands
the way I use them.
Make use of the hopeless flights
of tiresome pigeons
and this worn pebble, the only one
still sticking out from the water,
the way I use it.
Make use of the numb legs
on their way under water,
and the fear there's no way out,
the way I use it.
Make use of my impending death
the way I use it
just to hear the whisper
between us, preferably
made of ordinary words.

HOW YOU FALL IN LOVE (2012)

In love with my
future,
I've always dreaded
being caught
one day breeding
an incestuous dream.
In truth, nothing
like this has ever
happened between us,
even though
the tension seemed
mutual like
the age gap.
Only a new love can
cure the old one, I
keep repeating to myself
when picking up
lentils from the ashes
in such moments. Seed
after seed after seed after
seed . . .

When you fall in love
with your past,
an old man is born
inside yourself, whose
hands of yours shake,
whose legs of yours
hurt, finding it hard
to climb out of your
bed. At times, you're
a bit impatient
with the annoying
guest, but nothing can
stop a woman
in love. And when
my darling realizes it,
he vanishes like a book
among books.
Nobody touches it
for centuries,
only the air dries
its rounded back
until it ignites
in a fire to be
remembered for many
millennia to come.

How can you
fall in love with
your daughter?

You just catch sight of her
becoming lively,
naked in the room,
between a dress and
a dress, and the bellybutton
on her skin
shining up so you can
no longer breathe faced with
her freedom.
Then you make use
of every possible technique
of inconspicuous
disappearance for her,
so wholesome,
not to worry about
her mother crying.

When you fall in love
with your mother,
she's awake again
when she should be
asleep, so
you become her
mother, hoping
to finally get
enough sleep.

When you fall in love
with your father,
he still doesn't
have a clue
he's your greatest
love.

When you fall in love
with your sister,
a tree grows up
in America,
knowing
your births.
When the first and
the last quarters
wheel the world
in halves,
the red bark,
the red branches, and
the turquoise leaves
are impressed
into the soft wax
of your moons.
You don't have to
go to America.
You know it.

When you fall in love
with your brother,
you realize you
don't have a brother,
and you start to look
for one everywhere.
Even when
setting out on long
journeys,
you're dressed up
as the eldest,
the middle, and
the youngest sons.
Sometimes alone,
sometimes in threes,
on your every road,
on every walk,
at every turn
home from school,
you look for your
brother. On finding
him, you're
safe
forever.

When you fall in love
with your dog,
you put on his
yellow paws
and run off
with his
swift heart
from friend to
friend, from
neighbor to
neighbor, from
stranger to
stranger.
On drawing
a picture of all
his routes,
you can lay
your tired head
on the doormat
of a healed world.

How do you fall in love
with a human?

You watch again and again,
contemplate him throughout
the years and the days, night and
day, through births
and deaths,
the dead and the killed,
through men and
women, through children,
through children,
through the rain and through
rocks, you watch.
You watch. Even once
your eyes have ceased
to watch, you watch.

When I fall in love
with my mistakes,
I'm one big
mistake.
There's nothing
else up here
nor down there,
not even
in between.
It feels
like the outburst
of freedom,
only much
wittier.
I could have
smiled
earlier.

How can you
fall in love with your
death?

You gently peel your
lips, your cheeks, and
your nasal cartilage
off your face. Once
your teeth start to fall out,
you mourn each and
every one of them, and when
your living tongue slides
through the lower jaw,
you intercept it
affectionately. It feels
better now, yet until
you've put down your eyes,
you feel disturbed by the color
of the rolling oranges
and the sensation of a miracle
in the succession of their
collisions. At the same time, you're
troubled by the second movement
of the seventh symphony
and, most of all, by the fear
of not being able to recognize
silence. The silence starts
listing everybody

you've cheated on with your
new infatuation, and once
you're filled with the warmth
of their touches, you begin
to tremble. Not with your body, it's
your trembling you're trembling with
as if it were eternity
that was trembling. Trembling,
you suddenly remember
the words, any words or those
saying nobody becomes
better just by
being dead. Then you start
to calm down and even
manage to keep still, knowing
you'll never
get any rest.

When you outgrow
your travel sickness
and finally fall
in love with your
traveling, you
no longer travel.
You just agree on
who's going to play
the Indians, and
enjoy the game
until the night falls
in the early summer,
when, flushed and sweaty,
you're called home
for supper.

In love with
your being in love,
you're not real.
Floods of red blood
are bought
in the theater outlet,
even the leg
they cut off you
without anesthesia,
is only tied, just like
this, to your
unreal back.
Not even death
will make you
real, regardless
of how dearly
you pay for its
engagement.

If I fell in love
with myself, I'd demolish
within a second every scaly
wall, every spiral
staircase, every creaky
house and unfinished
construction, even the grand
system of the royal
underground would I demolish.

If I fell in love
with myself, I'd slowly
erase the picture
of my body,
leaving my pale face
in the grainy
photo of the deceased.

In love with myself, I'd find
it hard to draw the line between
myself and yourselves. I'd keep
crossing it, more alive
than ever before.

Do I love you beyond
your suiting me?
Do I love you when
you don't suit me?
Can I, when you
don't suit me, love
you beyond
my desire you'd
suit me someday?
Will you or will you
not shut my mouth
with a kiss?

DISAPPOINTMENT I

I've clung on to you.
It feels nice.
A friend told me
disappointment
is a good start.
Your friend is
wise.
I've hated him since.

DISAPPOINTMENT II

As long as there's no room
for disappointment, there's
no room for you, you say.

All the less for me
as I'm going to
disappoint you to the bone,
to the very holes around
its disappointed
marrow.

It's easier for me
now that you
know it.

THE RIVER I

There are ten delights
I know of
in the middle flow.

The first one.
When the undividable is
being divided against the rock,
with no ending
neither is there a cut.

The second one.
When we form white foam
on the other side of the rock
and hug differently
each time even though
the two of us haven't broken up.

The third one.
When a drop of rain makes its way
into myself without touching,
leaving there
a clear trace.

The fourth one.
When a crumbled rain
combs through my skin
as though I had it.

The fifth one.
When the audible voice
isn't mine,
but the song of moist in the moth
is.

The sixth one.
When it's really moist,
with the place I breathe in
being everywhere.

The seventh one.
When the child checks
whether it's raining
on the other window as well.

The eighth one.
When I'm puzzled
myself too.

The ninth one.
When I'm there.

The tenth one.
When I'm not.

THE HEART

The heart on my side
is purring and the heart
on your side is also purring.
No one can stay
serious when hearing
a heart purr, especially
not you wanting to lie
on my side.

We may pop off
from the happy laughter,
we may be found
perfectly dead
while perfectly healthy
since nothing
is healthier than a heart
that purrs.

THE MEMORY

In chocolate
I no longer taste chocolate,
but the memory
of its pieces tentatively
portioned out and the aroma
escaping from the cupboard
with the better glasses
being taken out.
And in the first cherries
I don't seek this summer
but lie in wait
for the round smoothness,
the innocent flavorless
flavor becoming
shorter and shorter.
And for me
the ice cream is wasted
for good.

Love, though,
eludes me for exactly
the opposite reason.
I can't
recall it.

THE DOG

The faithful fear
of me only
dreaming,
this dog is lying
under the table,
gnawing at
its bloody ankle.

LADYBIRDS

Until this spring, it had seemed
that I wasn't going to wear
such red dresses anymore, yet
ladybirds are blooming from
this mild winter everywhere.

I'm blowing
into their wings,
making them fall,
fall along my skirt
into your hair.

THE SQUIRRELS

The heartbeat
of the two frightened
squirrels having found
a hollow for the night
and who even fell asleep
for a moment
after the ardent loving,
later jumping, almost
simultaneously,
from the nightmare
into the cold perspiration
of an almost similar
half-awake state,
their fleeing heart
unable to settle down,
yet the moving softness
of an inseparable pelt
saved them
for some more time
into the same night.

THE SEAGULL AND THE CLOUD

The cloud on my daughter's
drawing seemed to be
imitating the seagull flying
above it, especially its
wing. It was just the
opposite, of course, yet
it would be too easy to
trust the clouds,
withholding some of
our gestures, the
pictures of white
airplanes and
the seagull.
I cannot yet
rely on
a child's
wing.

ALL OF A SUDDEN

The first breath of
wind chose the poem
on the table only just
written, just one,
and carried it away
in an arc.

I was looking for it,
a rectangular of whiteness
on the red roof, a white
sheet on the dark
grass behind the house
and in the brown fields
still further away

until the first drops and for
some more time into the rain.

FOR YOU

The great desire
this poem written for
you to be so beautiful
to leave people
breathless and
make asthmatics
die and
the best poets
bite their
quills in half
since nothing else
can be written,
this strong desire
has ruined quite
a few of my good
poems.

THE SYNDROME

Some people are
dizzied by Florence.
I myself find it hard to
endure the color of the
Soča. When the sun shines,
it reflects moonlight.

WETLANDS AT DUSK

The rustling, as
dense as dense are
the reeds within,

the voicelessness of the wind
above the water's surface, as clear-cut
as outlined by the rustling edge,

the chirrup of a little bird in
turquoise flight and the vague splash
of the egret's little black leg,

this is what silence is.

THE GAZE

The sea is now
much more
silvery. Everything
is subsiding somehow,
especially the taste
of tomatoes, while
the sea is becoming
much more
silvery.
The waves
are being stirred like
flocks of small heads
jumping under the
sheet, and it's not
advisable to avert your
gaze because, at that
very moment, the heads
sink under the backs of
the bright little fish,
under the living skin
so silvery as to show
on the horizon as
white.

A CRANNY

Only a hair
of a sort on the white
wall at first,
a creased membrane
of the plaster, then
slowly, slowly a crack
that the little finger
can measure.

We're looking at
each other, breathing.
Watchful, as though
it can open. Nothing

is definite, just
a slurping feeling,
and now a concern
that all my oddities
are to be joined by
this shallow
breathing through
a cranny.

LUCK

Most of my problems
have to do with luck. It
swaggers about my house,
shifting my objects,
especially the paperweights,
every day it acts out
an earthquake and the end
of the world, so now I
understand why some
people, when luck knocks
on their door, prefer to get
sick, close the shutters,
and die.

With luck,
it's either luck or the house.
It wouldn't let me keep
anything else either.
The sorrowful pillar of salt
I've hardly scratched
from earth doesn't exist.
Tiredness, not at all!
Incompetence,
what's that?

Luckily, I don't care
for the house or the
paperweights, not even
sorrow as much as it may
seem at times. I find it hard
to part with tiredness, with
incompetence, but
everything would still be
pretty much okay if only
I knew who now carries
my name and who now
enters and exits where
there is no house.

Is it possible for me to
be sold by accident
at some market? Could it
happen that my own
mother wouldn't
recognize me, just
offering me some tea
in surprise, sending me
away, with me thinking
she's right?

A MINUTE HEAD START (2015)

STRICTLY NECESSARY

I may have already written
what was strictly necessary and
will have to do something else now.
I feel kind of sorry and I'm a bit
shaken up if that's really the case.

Yet it seems unbearable
to imagine lapsing into a coma
or death one day
without telling you, not even
mentioning to you how it is now.

How one day, as I keep
waking up with you to days,
suddenly, gratitude emerged,
not only for you,
but for everything.

I'm yet to write this down.
I'm writing it now.

BUSES AND TRAINS

Again and again
I return to get my suitcase,
my poems, my notebooks . . .
And the buses and the trains
have just left
without me.

THE IN-BETWEEN TIME

Everything unavailable, this is
all freedom is measured with.
It has to be fully experienced,
the in-between time, when there's
no bed there anymore, nor canopies,
and the age of Sagittarius
hasn't really arrived yet either.
This is where one needs to stop,
to breathe in the in-between air
and not to rush into what's to come.
As long as I have children,
I don't discuss freedom.
This is my time, the time
in between two wars,
and no disaster,
no end of the world,
no assumption
are of any concern to me.
My only chance is the time
of the tents in the backyard,
the water in the cans and
the door-to-door knocking.

ON THE WAY

The green water is
hindering my legs
and the vague purpose,
but it seems I need
to change the pills for
the cheaper ones and only
a little worse than these.
There's nobody in the elevator.
The nurse on duty
in the corridor thinks
the pills are for me,
putting on the face.
There's no harm done
in changing one illusion
for the other, she says,
ignoring the hall
having bent, twisting
now like a dark blue
water slide.

THE PERSON WALKING THE ROPE I

The same rope
untangled from
the dusty macramé
of my head,
loosened from my hands,
untwisted off the neck,
the same thin rope
is hovering in the wind
from here to who-knows-where,
invisible unless
its profile
lights up
in the sun.

THE PERSON WALKING THE ROPE II

There are no ropewalkers
in my family,
even the fools
haven't been discussed,
only occasionally
somebody left,
hurting everybody.
Every morning
I step onto
an invisible rope—
three steps forward
and then back
with shopping
bags in my hands.

THE PERSON WALKING THE ROPE III

There's no evidence
confirming it's a deadly
undertaking, yet nobody
has ever come back.
No knowledge really
seems to help, even though
nobody has stepped onto the rope
without bad experience.
No courage endures
that long, yet I cannot
survive the course
of greatest fear.
I may not die,
but I'm dead.

A POEM

This isn't a metaphor,
it really is like this:

A tall birch scintillating
finely its feathers
like a flock of green fingers
imitating the rain.

Yet some leaves really do
fly away with the wind

on a journey,
obliquely,
slowly,
yellowy.

Dismissed with greatest
and highest ease.

THE POEM ABOUT A GIFT

Today I wished
for you to be a woman.
A few sets of amber earrings
were physically touching,
and a few bracelets
self-confidence incarnate,
whereas three necklaces
could shift you into another
body dimension.
Into an amber-skin body,
smooth and radiant with little
sunny spots
and with a thin stream
of silver holding all this
together so as not to burn.
Did you know that amber
could be green and blue too?
Are you listening to me at all?
How much I could have
delighted you today
were you a woman!

THE POEM ABOUT TWO CLOUDS

A pair of blurry clouds in the sky.
It's not crucial for the sky that
I'm watching it in Poland, but I find it
eerie having seen, a year ago
in Paris, their white and purple
reflection in the patch of azure
inside Claude Monet's green pond.

Something bursts between
the memory of the painting
and the painting of the present,
something else—like a distinct snap
at first, almost like a smack on the head,
then something in the throat, something
like a cursed *yes* word.

Still, everything takes place on the fringe
of the eye, on the edge of the skull, quickly
sinking into the misty occiput of doubt.

THE POEM ABOUT THE STONES ON A STRING

The little stones with a hole inside or two,
the trophies of a form from a sandy beach,
like butterflies after the butterfly hunt,
yet like stones that never run,
only turn their sides and their light,
their wet faces, the hidden hues, the shadows
in the corner of a void below themselves,
and this one, rather angular.

THE POEM ABOUT AN ORDER

When I was leaving, you had me
write a poem for you.
As though having a suit tailored,
something nobody needs nowadays.
As though having an embroidery made
with a lady confined to some other age.
As though not having me do anything at all,
but offering me something.

THE POEM ABOUT A WINDOW

It's built in at a slight angle
and too big for this wall.
The panes will never be clean again,
and there's so much brown paint
it's impossible to close it.
The small handle doesn't lift the iron
crosspiece, so a light semicircle
is scratched on the sill.
If a piece of the peeled paint gets driven
under your nail, it keeps festering for long.
It used to be blue, light blue.

THE POEM ABOUT A ZIPPER

is a poem about me
sewing an iron zipper
on the old denims,
about two shiny needles
having broken,
and a sewing machine
possessing a soul,
but it won't make it to heaven
'cause it's pissing me off on purpose.

THE SNAIL

I've slid all around your house.
My silvery trace
has ended this chapter
of your life.
When you found me
on the wall after the rain,
you didn't detach me,
you looked away.
How fast it is,
you said later
though you know
nothing about
the specific speed
of your own life.

THE SWAN

Just as you've
almost turned away,
I will fly across your
window overlooking
the green river.
I'll glide just above
the surface from the left to
the right along the stream.
At a single sweep
of my wing, still
half-turned away,
you'll feel
green
emptiness
among
the atoms
of your
body

and
the river
and the
window.

THE WOLVES

We'd slaughtered
the herd
before dawn, but
we ate nothing.

In the morning, the birds
don't sing in the places
where the wolfish
powerlessness is left lying.

You know this quiet
morning, that's why you smoke
on the balcony, wearing the same
track behind the door.

THE ANT

I've strayed. The adventure
has been enormous, especially since
I skidded off the windowsill.
Only completely lost
can I find the unexpected.
Your downward look can't even
make out my legs, so don't ask about
the purpose. The speck of dirt wandering
jerkily around isn't going to reveal God's plan
to you. The pattern of my search is random.
That's how the robotic vacuum cleaner works.
It ends up vacuuming everything all the way
from edge to edge and returns home.
My world is boundless, but
I'm bound to return.

THE HERMIT CRAB

No key
unlocks it.
There's no door,
no snail
operculum.
No chance
of scanning
a card,
no fingerprint.
No electric
doorbell to
jangle
the arrival
in the spiral
of home,
so the white knuckles
of knocking
slide off
onto the floor
like little stones.
Only the home
camera,
some other one,
has captured the shadow
of the slow
shifting
across the naked
seabed.

THE FISH

When we flash
our silvery hips
off
your window pane,
you fall silent,
as abandoned
as the invisible kisses
mutely
impressed on our
side of the glass.

A TITMOUSE

I've come into your garden
because you've got lots
of grips
for me to take sidelong
jumps onto the wall,
and here and there onto
the fence and up and down
onto the grass. Then
I dig up a seed
of a last year's sunflower,
but this is not it.
I've come here
because of your cat.
I don't know what
this means, I only know
it's not about the cat,
nor is it about me.

A FEAR

I can't fear
the unknown.
Death is fearsome
only where I
imagine it is.

There's only one fear—
the fear of repetition.
Inscribed in the body.

From the painful tooth
in the childhood to the strings
pulled by those up there,
not all that high
among us,

the bloody nerve,
the tooth nerve of cowardice,
buzzing.

INDIGNATION

It keeps going up
sharply
through the floors
of my breath.
It doesn't see anybody.
Everything's devastated.
It yells something.

I can hear
the rattling of a chain
and the iron echo
of an empty bucket.
It reverberates off
the walls of the well,
still going upward.

Deep down,
helplessness,
drowning.

THE TWINS

I never know which one does the talking,
because, both dressed impeccably, both
with their faces locked, they don't even differ
in the sweat above their upper lip.
With their tautological logic they're
only used to winning, only that *the Scared One*
pretends to care about me, whereas *the Smart One*
reaches higher—he's bet on
the likeliest. On the horse
of the burnt-down woods and the ruined
seeds, on the thickened greed
and the transparent children's famine,
on the horse of young rage caught in the nettings
of the owners of god and, most of all, on blood
which can only be stopped by—the lack of blood.
He'd be stupid to bet on the other side.
The Smart One would rather be dead than stupid,
the Scared One, however, thrives on such scenes.

LOST FOR WORDS

I removed the battery
from *the Cynical Man.*
It said plus and
minus. I haven't
given it back since.
When he dries up,
I'll take him
with me.

THE HUNTER-BEAST

I wouldn't have thought this of myself,
but when they prescribed me to
just have a rest for one minute, I
burst helplessly into tears. I'd never
been ordered anything crueler in my life.
What about the consequences! What will
you do to me, the *Great Persecutor*,
if I stop for one minute?
How will you humiliate me, beat me up,
chop me up, eat me up, bury me in black
dung? What have you done that
I fear you so much, hurrying before your
long rifle? You don't give me a minute,
not even a minute head start.

THE DRUMROLL REHEARSAL

Silently imagine
a symphonic orchestra
among the trees in the middle
of a forest. Think of a brown cello
stuck in the soft ground, the drums
scattered here and there, and the smooth
chopping block of the timpani.
Replace the golden edging
of the black tree trunks for the luster
of the stretched trombone
and do not overlook the shiver
of the violin bows alongside
the oak shoots. Be a robin
fluttering off onto a thin branch
of the flute, and a flutist
holding her breath.
Then breathe through all
the possible swaps,
replace the skins along with
the black varnish of the soil, and hope
for the silence of the crack.

Who are you?

I'm waiting for my lab results.
Until someone's had a look
at them,
all options are
open.

Who are you?

I'm sleepy.

Who are you?

I'd like some coffee.

Who are you?

I need love.

What?

I'd like you
to see me
after the coffee break.

Who?

I don't know.
There's nobody at the back.

Who are you?

My mother would caress
my back in the evening.
Now my back is
my largest love
organ.

What do you want to say?

I don't know.
It's still underway.

Who are you?

Some words
and the snowfulness of non-words
among them.

You don't really believe that!

It's the twenty-sixth of March
and it's snowing outside.
In slow motion.

Who are you?

Obstructing the view.

Who are you?

I've been dreaming
about the game
of Telephone.
The message contained
no words, just
one deep inspiration
and one expiration.

I'd still want you
to see me.

Here I am.

To see something
that doesn't match
by definition,
yet it's essential.

I'm still here.

Something pink
I'm ashamed of.

Who are you?

To see is enough.

From the outset,
it went its own way.
My pain threshold
caved in.
They called it sensitivity,
being spoiled and lazy.

Who are you?

For some time, it's okay if you
try hard, but later,
even the voices of strangers hurt,
so do animal stories,
war reports,
the light, the winter,
the stairs,
the neighbors, the wrecked nest,
some children,
the black woman at the bedside
while the parents are talking
in the kitchen,
the laughter . . .

And what then?

Disappearing is
the only solution

So you're not here?

I don't know.
Somebody aches.

I've got one third
of my body
extra weight.
That's more than one
leg of mine
and an arm,
and the question is
whether cellular
information
is expendable
when being so substantial.

Who are you?

The question is
who I don't want
to be.

Who are you?

I don't know.
Everyone mentioned
is here.

A CHILD AND OTHER PHENOMENA
(NEW POEMS)

BY THE SHORE

When the evening sea was burning
with the chilly turquoise-purple fire all the way
to the horizon, we, the tourists by the shore,
spoke at length about the proliferation of algae.
We also brought up global warming,
gazing at the thick fluorescent tarpaulin
which kept catching fire lengthwise
in the rhythm of concealed waves.
Anxiously pleased about the weird beauty,
we were talking away
the premonition of an unknown calamity.

THE BLACK SHIPS IN THE SKY

And we wait. We no longer feed animals.
We wait and wait for the day
our powerlessness is confirmed
and will win.

Marcin Świetlicki

The black ships in the sky and
the wind underneath their bellies.

A good or a bad sign?
What army, what phenomenon?

Shall I go closer or as far away as
possible, behind the apartment blocks

even though it seems apparent
to the eye they won't endure.

IN THE SQUARE

In the morning, we, the first strollers,
caught sight of a frozen sky
over the empty town square.
It was as unreal
as a picture with a pale pattern.
Boulders also took shape,
seized up there in the icy grip.
With the logic increasing,
the architecture overhead
began to loosen. It let out a shriek
and started to fall down in enormous
sharp fragments. The square was
buried under by the icy sprinkle.

BY THE WALL

In my dream, I'd steal
jewelry and eat it.
In the afternoon, awake,
with the sun hanging aslant,
I'd stand between the crystal
chandelier and the wall to
intercept the rainbow.

These were the rare moments
of my joy.

At the time of my death,
I intend to become lively.
The mournful ones may
expect some unusual
phenomena. Something to do
with jumping up, whining,
and small objects.

OVER THERE

The flaxen scent of the new window putty
that sweated just a little bit under my fingertips,
the sudden thrusts of the flowering bushes, the ones
with the blossoms of the mock orange and those
with the hidden blossoms I don't know the name of,
the new-mown lawn—the clover
and the plantain, I assume, and the scorching asphalt
after the summer rain, this scent! Just once,
one winter before the new year, a fleeting
taste of cardamom—though for many decades to come
I didn't know it was cardamom—these
states seemed to have absolutely nothing
to do with death, capable of grabbing me
by one hand and pulling me, alive and with my entire
body, over there, into the future, like raising an orphan
from a well.

AT THAT LONG MOMENT

The phosphorescent ball on the Christmas tree
came hovering into the dark like a white little spirit
soon after we'd turned off the light.
I wished to keep repeating
this magic till I'm tired of it
because, at that long moment, between the click
of the switch (we all went quiet as if it
weren't to appear had we talked)
and the first blur of the little ball in the night,
my heart would instantly shrink to swell
immediately afterwards in the face of something
even such a longing look couldn't restrain.

THE CANDLE

The yellow, dense tip
of the burning above the vault
of its own gray shadow in between,
and the invisible lower part, azure
only at times—this is the flame
restlessly circling
the curved black wick
with the red little eyeball
facing the frightening night.

ME TOO

I've got children too.
My daughter asks me to start writing
nothing but happy poems,
and I know not whether it would be
irresponsible or courageous
if I could.

THE HOSPITAL

I'm much lighter beneath the ceiling
and I can move by way of swimming.
Without really wanting to, I notice some dust
on the upper side of the lighting,
and the dusty wing of a big mosquito
glued in between the metal bars of the lights.
It's trembling in the breeze that doesn't exist. There's
only the buzzing of light and the sorrowful souls.

Far below, a child is lying on the bed.
Not until he'd stopped calling his mother
from within, I rose from the drained belly.
Rather than a century-old thirst,
it was the abandonment that hurt.
Now he's being waken up and his naked body
humiliated, yet no infusion can soak the lost trust.
There's no room for me in the dead body of fear.

I'll remain here, as did the mosquito wing.

FROM A HOSPITAL

A child cut out from a room,
from his parents' photo,
from his little crib
with a blanket rolled under.

The child in the casket of darkness,
tied to another bed, not moving,
shortening his breath,
remaining still until death.

The child sent back unexpectedly.
The midday light on the table,
mother waiting, the wiped floor fragrant.
The corpse slowly moving.

A HOROSCOPE

Dead children grow up in a second,
but never for real.
Sometimes they miss children's experience,
but sometimes they don't know
what to miss.

They tend to be sensible to cold and change,
but mainly they're frightened,
on permanent standby,
ashamed of cowardice.
Most of all, they're ashamed of their decaying
bodies they suppress into dream,
but they can look really nice at first glance.

They're kidnapped by love, beauty, and passion,
but never by joy.
They're convinced it's all due to a moment
of inattention in children's joy.
They pretend for people to keep them,
but their sadness destroys
their children and everyone who loves them.

They trust nobody to stay
and they don't trust adults
to know anything at all, which
some grown-ups can find irritating.

When not knowing they're dead,
they have difficulty in deciding or learning,
but they do know they can fly.

They trust themselves the least.
They move slowly, in constant
risk of leaving forever.
They're too tired to fear death,
but nobody in the world wishes
more desperately to belong here.

THE CARCASS

When your own corpse wants
to enter your living room,
you don't embrace it, of course,
as your own. With infallible disgust
at everything ugly, you try to shut
the door, thinking even of the police.

Surprised by the frailty
of the large body, fearing
an infectious touch, you let her go by.
Unkempt, grimy, weak-minded,
decomposing, brown, blackish brown.

You don't know whose anger it is nor
who feels it, but shame can't stop it
as the creature heads toward the armchairs.
In unjust satisfaction, you think:
"There's mother sitting. Let them make a deal
in case one has to live with this."

A CHILD I

She surely is a child.
At times, she's three
or even less, at times
six or even eight.

She has the power of a horse
pulling two wagons,
harboring no doubt
about needing to pull them.

She imagines herself
as a large dead
and decaying mass.
She has no other idea.

Yet she feels herself to be
something small,
naked and exposed.
So she prefers not to feel.

She runs her own
concentration camp
she's locked in.
She manages the world there.

She paints fences, picks up
candy wrappers, divides people,

in general terms,
into the good and the bad guys.

She disables the bad guys,
distributes goods
and cleans the oceans.
Then she's tired.

A CHILD II

She hates God.
If God had a target in the middle
of his forehead, she'd strike him
one-handed and blow
the smoke from the barrel.

This shouldn't have happened to her,
every child knows it,
but it did, and it keeps happening
to others also, again and again.

So nobody should say to her
that anything is arranged,
that anything is in place
and meaningful because it's not,
any child can see this.

If only animals or trees
at least were exempt from this,
at least men or women,
or old people when the skin is thin.
Children, or toddlers at least.

It was her choice.
She could hate people
and stay aloud in the world,
yet being like this, godless,
she still can't join them.

A CHILD III

It's a topsy-turvy world,
where a child has to take care
that everything doesn't suddenly
come to its end,
and they could abandon him again
like moonwalkers
unable even to take care of themselves.
And, most of all, that the war doesn't come,
already standing at the doorstep.
It's a topsy-turvy world with only him
finding it unbearable that, at this moment,
children are burning in some war.
His heart is about to burst, so
he's learned to think only about himself,
that's why he does everything right
sharpening color pencils and putting them
into the box according to the color scale.
It's a topsy-turvy world
with everything being up to him.

HOW CONVENIENT

I haven't had a TV set for years. I don't want
to watch it so I don't get damaged. Besides,
how convenient it is that I don't have to see
the drowned in the beautiful Mediterranean.
A child with his little shoes, a child with his leg
rolled under. One among the rocks, bobbing like
seaweed, and this one with his face in the sand.

I prefer watching cute animals on the Net,
carefully selecting videos to avoid anything
that could upset me. For instance, I watch the bear
being recorded in the ZOO by a Slovenian family
and, quite unexpectedly, a young crow drowning
in his pond. It's still beating its wings, but
they're wet, not coming off the dirty water.

The bear slowly approaches it as though he
might well have done something else. When he
swings his heavy paw, we're positive he's about
to kill it, but he only gets hold of it carefully
with his paw and his snout, lifting it onto dry land.
"He's saved it," says the cameraman's wife
when the bird recovers.

IN THE BACKGROUND

In Taiwan, probably at a fish market,
a yellow dog has been recorded wanting
to save the fish from dying on the floor.
In the background, one can hear a surprised
laughter of the cameramen. They find
it cute to see the dog running from fish
to fish, touching their heads with its snout,
tirelessly pushing the water from the puddle
onto the helpless fish bodies with its muzzle.
The dog seems surprised, too, hardly
managing to look up toward the camera.
How is it possible he knows it
and we don't?

A LOVE POEM

It's true what they say, it's easier
to do minor things you can handle
than the major ones in an uncertainty
over the outcome. It's easier
to tidy up the house a little bit more,
later, it's dinnertime anyway.

I keep writing some other poem
every time, another one before
the right one. I find it easier even to write
about death, despite a distinct feeling
I want to write about the two of us, to

reach into the depth of all
the worn-out love lines, pulling out
the single one
and then another single one and so on
until I end up lying, as exhausted as
after a long, merciless love-making.

MAJA VIDMAR (b. 1961) has published seven poetry collections since *Body Distances* (1984), including *Presence*, which was awarded the prestigous Jenko Award in 2005 and the Prešeren Foundation Award in 2006. In 2015, she received the Velenjica–Cup of Immortality for outstanding poetic work of the last decade. She is the laureate of three international prizes, with seven poetry selections published in translation throughout Europe, and more than 70 contributions appearing in anthologies around the world.

ANDREJ PLETERSKI (b. 1979) is an award-winning literary translator from English, French, and Slovak, as well as of Slovenian poetry into English and Slovak. In addition to numerous contributions to literary journals and catalogues, he has published more than fifteen book-length translations and compiled three anthologies.

MICHAL AJVAZ, *The Golden Age.*
The Other City.
PIERRE ALBERT-BIROT, *Grabinoulor.*
YUZ ALESHKOVSKY, *Kangaroo.*
FELIPE ALFAU, *Chromos.*
Locos.
JOE AMATO, *Samuel Taylor's Last Night.*
IVAN ÂNGELO, *The Celebration.*
The Tower of Glass.
ANTÓNIO LOBO ANTUNES, *Knowledge of Hell.*
The Splendor of Portugal.
ALAIN ARIAS-MISSON, *Theatre of Incest.*
JOHN ASHBERY & JAMES SCHUYLER, *A Nest of Ninnies.*
ROBERT ASHLEY, *Perfect Lives.*
GABRIELA AVIGUR-ROTEM, *Heatwave and Crazy Birds.*
DJUNA BARNES, *Ladies Almanack.*
Ryder.
JOHN BARTH, *Letters.*
Sabbatical.
DONALD BARTHELME, *The King.*
Paradise.
SVETISLAV BASARA, *Chinese Letter.*
MIQUEL BAUÇÀ, *The Siege in the Room.*
RENÉ BELLETTO, *Dying.*
MAREK BIENCZYK, *Transparency.*
ANDREI BITOV, *Pushkin House.*
ANDREJ BLATNIK, *You Do Understand.*
Law of Desire.
LOUIS PAUL BOON, *Chapel Road.*
My Little War.
Summer in Termuren.
ROGER BOYLAN, *Killoyle.*
IGNÁCIO DE LOYOLA BRANDÃO, *Anonymous Celebrity.*
Zero.
BONNIE BREMSER, *Troia: Mexican Memoirs.*
CHRISTINE BROOKE-ROSE, *Amalgamemnon.*
BRIGID BROPHY, *In Transit.*
The Prancing Novelist.

GERALD L. BRUNS, *Modern Poetry and the Idea of Language.*
GABRIELLE BURTON, *Heartbreak Hotel.*
MICHEL BUTOR, *Degrees.*
Mobile.
G. CABRERA INFANTE, *Infante's Inferno.*
Three Trapped Tigers.
JULIETA CAMPOS, *The Fear of Losing Eurydice.*
ANNE CARSON, *Eros the Bittersweet.*
ORLY CASTEL-BLOOM, *Dolly City.*
LOUIS-FERDINAND CÉLINE, *North.*
Conversations with Professor Y.
London Bridge.
MARIE CHAIX, *The Laurels of Lake Constance.*
HUGO CHARTERIS, *The Tide Is Right.*
ERIC CHEVILLARD, *Demolishing Nisard.*
The Author and Me.
MARC CHOLODENKO, *Mordechai Schamz.*
JOSHUA COHEN, *Witz.*
EMILY HOLMES COLEMAN, *The Shutter of Snow.*
ERIC CHEVILLARD, *The Author and Me.*
ROBERT COOVER, *A Night at the Movies.*
STANLEY CRAWFORD, *Log of the S.S. The Mrs Unguentine.*
Some Instructions to My Wife.
RENÉ CREVEL, *Putting My Foot in It.*
RALPH CUSACK, *Cadenza.*
NICHOLAS DELBANCO, *Sherbrookes.*
The Count of Concord.
NIGEL DENNIS, *Cards of Identity.*
PETER DIMOCK, *A Short Rhetoric for Leaving the Family.*
ARIEL DORFMAN, *Konfidenz.*
COLEMAN DOWELL, *Island People.*
Too Much Flesh and Jabez.
ARKADII DRAGOMOSHCHENKO, *Dust.*
RIKKI DUCORNET, *Phosphor in Dreamland.*
The Complete Butcher's Tales.

RIKKI DUCORNET (cont.), *The Jade Cabinet.*
The Fountains of Neptune.
WILLIAM EASTLAKE, *The Bamboo Bed.*
Castle Keep.
Lyric of the Circle Heart.
JEAN ECHENOZ, *Chopin's Move.*
STANLEY ELKIN, *A Bad Man.*
Criers and Kibitzers, Kibitzers and Criers.
The Dick Gibson Show.
The Franchiser.
The Living End.
Mrs. Ted Bliss.
FRANÇOIS EMMANUEL, *Invitation to a Voyage.*
PAUL EMOND, *The Dance of a Sham.*
SALVADOR ESPRIU, *Ariadne in the Grotesque Labyrinth.*
LESLIE A. FIEDLER, *Love and Death in the American Novel.*
JUAN FILLOY, *Op Oloop.*
ANDY FITCH, *Pop Poetics.*
GUSTAVE FLAUBERT, *Bouvard and Pécuchet.*
KASS FLEISHER, *Talking out of School.*
JON FOSSE, *Aliss at the Fire.*
Melancholy.
FORD MADOX FORD, *The March of Literature.*
MAX FRISCH, *I'm Not Stiller.*
Man in the Holocene.
CARLOS FUENTES, *Christopher Unborn.*
Distant Relations.
Terra Nostra.
Where the Air Is Clear.
TAKEHIKO FUKUNAGA, *Flowers of Grass.*
WILLIAM GADDIS, JR., *The Recognitions.*
JANICE GALLOWAY, *Foreign Parts.*
The Trick Is to Keep Breathing.
WILLIAM H. GASS, *Life Sentences.*
The Tunnel.
The World Within the Word.
Willie Masters' Lonesome Wife.
GÉRARD GAVARRY, *Hoppla! 1 2 3.*

ETIENNE GILSON, *The Arts of the Beautiful.*
Forms and Substances in the Arts.
C. S. GISCOMBE, *Giscome Road.*
Here.
DOUGLAS GLOVER, *Bad News of the Heart.*
WITOLD GOMBROWICZ, *A Kind of Testament.*
PAULO EMÍLIO SALES GOMES, *P's Three Women.*
GEORGI GOSPODINOV, *Natural Novel.*
JUAN GOYTISOLO, *Count Julian.*
Juan the Landless.
Makbara.
Marks of Identity.
HENRY GREEN, *Blindness.*
Concluding.
Doting.
Nothing.
JACK GREEN, *Fire the Bastards!*
JIŘÍ GRUŠA, *The Questionnaire.*
MELA HARTWIG, *Am I a Redundant Human Being?*
JOHN HAWKES, *The Passion Artist.*
Whistlejacket.
ELIZABETH HEIGHWAY, ED., *Contemporary Georgian Fiction.*
AIDAN HIGGINS, *Balcony of Europe.*
Blind Man's Bluff.
Bornholm Night-Ferry.
Langrishe, Go Down.
Scenes from a Receding Past.
KEIZO HINO, *Isle of Dreams.*
KAZUSHI HOSAKA, *Plainsong.*
ALDOUS HUXLEY, *Antic Hay.*
Point Counter Point.
Those Barren Leaves.
Time Must Have a Stop.
NAOYUKI II, *The Shadow of a Blue Cat.*
DRAGO JANČAR, *The Tree with No Name.*
MIKHEIL JAVAKHISHVILI, *Kvachi.*
GERT JONKE, *The Distant Sound.*
Homage to Czerny.
The System of Vienna.

JACQUES JOUET, *Mountain R.*
Savage.
Upstaged.
MIEKO KANAI, *The Word Book.*
YORAM KANIUK, *Life on Sandpaper.*
ZURAB KARUMIDZE, *Dagny.*
JOHN KELLY, *From Out of the City.*
HUGH KENNER, *Flaubert, Joyce and Beckett: The Stoic Comedians.*
Joyce's Voices.
DANILO KIŠ, *The Attic.*
The Lute and the Scars.
Psalm 44.
A Tomb for Boris Davidovich.
ANITA KONKKA, *A Fool's Paradise.*
GEORGE KONRÁD, *The City Builder.*
TADEUSZ KONWICKI, *A Minor Apocalypse.*
The Polish Complex.
ANNA KORDZAIA-SAMADASHVILI, *Me, Margarita.*
MENIS KOUMANDAREAS, *Koula.*
ELAINE KRAF, *The Princess of 72nd Street.*
JIM KRUSOE, *Iceland.*
AYSE KULIN, *Farewell: A Mansion in Occupied Istanbul.*
EMILIO LASCANO TEGUI, *On Elegance While Sleeping.*
ERIC LAURRENT, *Do Not Touch.*
VIOLETTE LEDUC, *La Bâtarde.*
EDOUARD LEVÉ, *Autoportrait.*
Newspaper.
Suicide.
Works.
MARIO LEVI, *Istanbul Was a Fairy Tale.*
DEBORAH LEVY, *Billy and Girl.*
JOSÉ LEZAMA LIMA, *Paradiso.*
ROSA LIKSOM, *Dark Paradise.*
OSMAN LINS, *Avalovara.*
The Queen of the Prisons of Greece.
FLORIAN LIPUŠ, *The Errors of Young Tjaž.*
GORDON LISH, *Peru.*
ALF MACLOCHLAINN, *Out of Focus.*
Past Habitual.

The Corpus in the Library.
RON LOEWINSOHN, *Magnetic Field(s).*
YURI LOTMAN, *Non-Memoirs.*
D. KEITH MANO, *Take Five.*
MINA LOY, *Stories and Essays of Mina Loy.*
MICHELINE AHARONIAN MARCOM, *A Brief History of Yes.*
The Mirror in the Well.
BEN MARCUS, *The Age of Wire and String.*
WALLACE MARKFIELD, *Teitlebaum's Window.*
DAVID MARKSON, *Reader's Block.*
Wittgenstein's Mistress.
CAROLE MASO, *AVA.*
HISAKI MATSUURA, *Triangle.*
LADISLAV MATEJKA & KRYSTYNA POMORSKA, EDS., *Readings in Russian Poetics: Formalist & Structuralist Views.*
HARRY MATHEWS, *Cigarettes.*
The Conversions.
The Human Country.
The Journalist.
My Life in CIA.
Singular Pleasures.
The Sinking of the Odradek.
Stadium.
Tlooth.
HISAKI MATSUURA, *Triangle.*
DONAL MCLAUGHLIN, *beheading the virgin mary, and other stories.*
JOSEPH MCELROY, *Night Soul and Other Stories.*
ABDELWAHAB MEDDEB, *Talismano.*
GERHARD MEIER, *Isle of the Dead.*
HERMAN MELVILLE, *The Confidence-Man.*
AMANDA MICHALOPOULOU, *I'd Like.*
STEVEN MILLHAUSER, *The Barnum Museum.*
In the Penny Arcade.
RALPH J. MILLS, JR., *Essays on Poetry.*
MOMUS, *The Book of Jokes.*
CHRISTINE MONTALBETTI, *The Origin of Man.*
Western.

NICHOLAS MOSLEY, *Accident.*
Assassins.
Catastrophe Practice.
A Garden of Trees.
Hopeful Monsters.
Imago Bird.
Inventing God.
Look at the Dark.
Metamorphosis.
Natalie Natalia.
Serpent.
WARREN MOTTE, *Fables of the Novel: French Fiction since 1990.*
Fiction Now: The French Novel in the 21st Century.
Mirror Gazing.
Oulipo: A Primer of Potential Literature.
GERALD MURNANE, *Barley Patch.*
Inland.
YVES NAVARRE, *Our Share of Time.*
Sweet Tooth.
DOROTHY NELSON, *In Night's City.*
Tar and Feathers.
ESHKOL NEVO, *Homesick.*
WILFRIDO D. NOLLEDO, *But for the Lovers.*
BORIS A. NOVAK, *The Master of Insomnia.*
FLANN O'BRIEN, *At Swim-Two-Birds.*
The Best of Myles.
The Dalkey Archive.
The Hard Life.
The Poor Mouth.
The Third Policeman.
CLAUDE OLLIER, *The Mise-en-Scène.*
Wert and the Life Without End.
PATRIK OUŘEDNÍK, *Europeana.*
The Opportune Moment, 1855.
BORIS PAHOR, *Necropolis.*
FERNANDO DEL PASO, *News from the Empire.*
Palinuro of Mexico.
ROBERT PINGET, *The Inquisitory.*
Mahu or The Material.
Trio.
MANUEL PUIG, *Betrayed by Rita Hayworth.*

The Buenos Aires Affair.
Heartbreak Tango.
RAYMOND QUENEAU, *The Last Days.*
Odile.
Pierrot Mon Ami.
Saint Glinglin.
ANN QUIN, *Berg.*
Passages.
Three.
Tripticks.
ISHMAEL REED, *The Free-Lance Pallbearers.*
The Last Days of Louisiana Red.
Ishmael Reed: The Plays.
Juice!
The Terrible Threes.
The Terrible Twos.
Yellow Back Radio Broke-Down.
JASIA REICHARDT, *15 Journeys Warsaw to London.*
JOÃO UBALDO RIBEIRO, *House of the Fortunate Buddhas.*
JEAN RICARDOU, *Place Names.*
RAINER MARIA RILKE,
The Notebooks of Malte Laurids Brigge.
JULIÁN RÍOS, *The House of Ulysses.*
Larva: A Midsummer Night's Babel.
Poundemonium.
ALAIN ROBBE-GRILLET, *Project for a Revolution in New York.*
A Sentimental Novel.
AUGUSTO ROA BASTOS, *I the Supreme.*
DANIËL ROBBERECHTS, *Arriving in Avignon.*
JEAN ROLIN, *The Explosion of the Radiator Hose.*
OLIVIER ROLIN, *Hotel Crystal.*
ALIX CLEO ROUBAUD, *Alix's Journal.*
JACQUES ROUBAUD, *The Form of a City Changes Faster, Alas, Than the Human Heart.*
The Great Fire of London.
Hortense in Exile.
Hortense Is Abducted.
Mathematics: The Plurality of Worlds of Lewis.
Some Thing Black.

RAYMOND ROUSSEL, *Impressions of Africa.*

VEDRANA RUDAN, *Night.*

PABLO M. RUIZ, *Four Cold Chapters on the Possibility of Literature.*

GERMAN SADULAEV, *The Maya Pill.*

TOMAŽ ŠALAMUN, *Soy Realidad.*

LYDIE SALVAYRE, *The Company of Ghosts.*
The Lecture.
The Power of Flies.

LUIS RAFAEL SÁNCHEZ, *Macho Camacho's Beat.*

SEVERO SARDUY, *Cobra & Maitreya.*

NATHALIE SARRAUTE, *Do You Hear Them?*
Martereau.
The Planetarium.

STIG SÆTERBAKKEN, *Siamese.*
Self-Control.
Through the Night.

ARNO SCHMIDT, *Collected Novellas.*
Collected Stories.
Nobodaddy's Children.
Two Novels.

ASAF SCHURR, *Motti.*

GAIL SCOTT, *My Paris.*

DAMION SEARLS, *What We Were Doing and Where We Were Going.*

JUNE AKERS SEESE, *Is This What Other Women Feel Too?*

BERNARD SHARE, *Inish.*
Transit.

VIKTOR SHKLOVSKY, *Bowstring.*
Literature and Cinematography.
Theory of Prose.
Third Factory.
Zoo, or Letters Not about Love.

PIERRE SINIAC, *The Collaborators.*

KJERSTI A. SKOMSVOLD, *The Faster I Walk, the Smaller I Am.*

JOSEF ŠKVORECKÝ, *The Engineer of Human Souls.*

GILBERT SORRENTINO, *Aberration of Starlight.*
Blue Pastoral.
Crystal Vision.

Imaginative Qualities of Actual Things.
Mulligan Stew. Red the Fiend.
Steelwork.
Under the Shadow.

MARKO SOSIČ, *Ballerina, Ballerina.*

ANDRZEJ STASIUK, *Dukla.*
Fado.

GERTRUDE STEIN, *The Making of Americans.*
A Novel of Thank You.

LARS SVENDSEN, *A Philosophy of Evil.*

PIOTR SZEWC, *Annihilation.*

GONÇALO M. TAVARES, *A Man: Klaus Klump.*
Jerusalem.
Learning to Pray in the Age of Technique.

LUCIAN DAN TEODOROVICI, *Our Circus Presents...*

NIKANOR TERATOLOGEN, *Assisted Living.*

STEFAN THEMERSON, *Hobson's Island.*
The Mystery of the Sardine.
Tom Harris.

TAEKO TOMIOKA, *Building Waves.*

JOHN TOOMEY, *Sleepwalker.*

DUMITRU TSEPENEAG, *Hotel Europa.*
The Necessary Marriage.
Pigeon Post.
Vain Art of the Fugue.

ESTHER TUSQUETS, *Stranded.*

DUBRAVKA UGRESIC, *Lend Me Your Character.*
Thank You for Not Reading.

TOR ULVEN, *Replacement.*

MATI UNT, *Brecht at Night.*
Diary of a Blood Donor.
Things in the Night.

ÁLVARO URIBE & OLIVIA SEARS, EDS., *Best of Contemporary Mexican Fiction.*

ELOY URROZ, *Friction.*
The Obstacles.

LUISA VALENZUELA, *Dark Desires and the Others.*
He Who Searches.

PAUL VERHAEGHEN, *Omega Minor.*

BORIS VIAN, *Heartsnatcher.*

LLORENÇ VILLALONGA, *The Dolls' Room.*

TOOMAS VINT, *An Unending Landscape.*

ORNELA VORPSI, *The Country Where No One Ever Dies.*

AUSTRYN WAINHOUSE, *Hedyphagetica.*

CURTIS WHITE, *America's Magic Mountain.*
The Idea of Home.
Memories of My Father Watching TV.
Requiem.

DIANE WILLIAMS,
Excitability: Selected Stories.
Romancer Erector.

DOUGLAS WOOLF, *Wall to Wall.*
Ya! & John-Juan.

JAY WRIGHT, *Polynomials and Pollen.*
The Presentable Art of Reading Absence.

PHILIP WYLIE, *Generation of Vipers.*

MARGUERITE YOUNG, *Angel in the Forest.*
Miss MacIntosh, My Darling.

REYOUNG, *Unbabbling.*

VLADO ŽABOT, *The Succubus.*

ZORAN ŽIVKOVIĆ , *Hidden Camera.*

LOUIS ZUKOFSKY, *Collected Fiction.*

VITOMIL ZUPAN, *Minuet for Guitar.*

SCOTT ZWIREN, *God Head.*

AND MORE . . .